Supporting Bereaved and Dying Children and Their Parents

by
Martin Herbert

BPS BOOKS THE BRITISH PSYCHOLOGICAL SOCIETY

First published in 1996 by BPS Books (The British Psychological Society), St Andrews House, 48 Princess Road East, Leicester LE1 7DR, UK.

A catalogue record for this book is available from the British Library.

ISBN 1 85433 187 6

Typeset by Ralph Footring, Derby.

Reprinted 1999

Contents

Supporting bereaved and dying children and their parents

Introduction

> *The death of a child 'upturns the natural order of things'. We expect old people to die one day, but no parent is ready to accept the death of a child cut off by an accident or illness from all their dreams and aspirations.*

(From Ward *et al.*, 1993)

Aims

The aim of this guide is to provide bereavement counsellors, nurses, doctors and other health care and social services professionals with knowledge, skills and values which will assist them in the daunting task of helping children and their families at a time of the deepest possible distress and uncertainty, and, to this end, to develop their understanding of how children and adults react to the loss, or imminent loss, of loved ones.

On the part of the practitioner, this will require:

➤ that practitioners are sensitive not only to the feelings, fears and (often) unspoken concerns of the persons in their care, but also to the personal and professional stresses and strains that are likely to reveal themselves in the course of this work;

➤ that there is an understanding of how children and adults (the surviving parents) react to the loss of loved ones;

➤ that practitioners can marshall the information, knowledge, skills and emotional resources a dying (or seriously ill) child or parent and his/her family are likely to need;

➤ that the practitioner appreciates what children understand by illness and death;

➤ that the practitioner can communicate honestly and intelligibly about subjects most people prefer not to talk about;

➤ that the practitioner appreciates that each disease presents specific problems to the child and family. They vary according to the nature, frequency, visibility and severity of symptoms, the degree to which they are disabling or life-threatening, and the demands of the necessary treatment;

➤ that the practitioner has skills and strategies to support bereaved individuals in their grief.

Pain and healing

Grief has been described as a 'mental wound' which heals slowly and leaves scars. If children (for whatever reason) are unable to 'work through' the period of grieving, they may suffer lasting emotional damage. The loss of a parent, for example, is one of the foremost precursors of depressive disorders. In order to help children cope with the loss of a parent, we need to understand how and when their reactions are both normal and necessary. In this sense, grief is not only a 'mental wound', it is also a *process* – a 'healing pain' that enables the child to experience a range of powerful emotions on their journey to making an emotional adjustment to life without the loved person.

Rob Long and Jenny Bates put it like this:

> To avoid parts of the journey, or to rush through will be unsatisfactory. Imagine for a moment you have cut yourself; you will expect your body to take time to heal itself. During this healing time there will be pain. A scar will form, and gradually new skin will grow underneath. Similarly, a loss is just such a wound to our emotional self, and we require a special time to experience the pain and heal.

This guide addresses itself to these two issues: the pain of bereavement and the means of helping children and other members of the family to heal.

Part I: When a child dies

The bonds of love

The death of a child is a particularly distressing event as it raises a range of feelings about lost hope, lost expectations, a lost future, and the loss of the child's faith in the parents' or the doctors' ability to protect and save them.

(Douglas, 1993).

All infants need to become attached to a parent (or parent substitute) in order to survive. The child's emotional tie to its parents and their bonding to him or her lie at the very foundation of normal development. One of the essential tasks of infancy is the development of a basic trust in others. During the early months and years of life, children learn whether the world is a good and satisfying place to live in, or a source of pain, misery, frustration and uncertainty. Because human infants are so totally dependent for so long, they need to know that they can depend on the outside world.

This is where Jo Douglas' words are so poignant. The separation of child and parents which is part of the pattern of serious illness – be it parent or child who goes into hospital, or is facing the ultimate separation of death – takes people to the far edge of suffering. Ralph Waldo Emerson observed perceptively that 'sorrow makes us all children again'.

Separation anxiety

A further turn of the screw comes from the potency of separation anxiety as part of the child's experience of normal (let alone disrupted) development. Children's fears show a clear pattern as they grow up and each age is to have its own set of 'adjustment' crises or anxieties. Studies of the behaviour of healthy children separated from their parents in the second and third years of life tend to show a fairly predictable sequence of behaviour. Their separation anxiety can be illustrated by a young child's mother going into hospital.

> In the first, or 'protest', stage children react to the separation with tears and anger. They demand their mother's return and seem

hopeful that they will succeed in getting her back. This stage may last several days.

➤   Later they become quieter, but it is clear that they are just as preoccupied with their absent mother and still yearn for her return. However, their hopes may have faded.

➤   This is called the phase of 'despair'. Often the stages alternate: hope turns to despair, and despair to renewed hope.

➤   Eventually a greater change occurs and children seem to forget their mother so that, when they see her again, they remain curiously uninterested in her and may seem not to recognize her.

➤   This is the so-called stage of 'detachment'.

In each of these phases children are prone to tantrums and episodes of destructive behaviour. After reunion with their parents, they may be unresponsive and undemanding and to what degree and for how long will depend on the length of the separation and whether or not the children made frequent visits to their mothers during that period. For example, if they have been deprived of visits for a good few weeks and have reached the early stages of detachment, it is likely that unresponsiveness will persist for varying periods, ranging from a few hours to several days. When at last this unresponsiveness subsides, the intense ambivalence of their feelings for their mother is made manifest. There is a storm of feeling, intense clinging, and whenever mother leaves them even for a moment, acute anxiety and rage. Here is the mother of a four-year-old speaking.

> Ever since I left her that time I had to go into hospital (two periods, 17 days each), my child doesn't trust me any more. I can't go anywhere – over to the neighbours' or to the shops. I've always got to take her. She wouldn't leave me. She went down to the school gates at dinner time today. She ran like mad home. She said, 'Oh Mam, I thought you was gone!' She can't forget it. She's still round me all the time. I just sit down and put her on my knee and love her. Definitely. If I don't do it, she says 'Mam, you don't love me any more'; I've *got* to sit down.

But what of the child who has to go to hospital with a serious illness or life-threatening injuries? The intimations and fears of separation are likely to be much greater. The preoccupations of the dying child may be twofold:

➤   they are upset at the thought of separation from their parents;

> they are apprehensive about heaven, what it will be like, how they will get there, will they be alone and so on.

The suffering, particularly the unspoken, uncomprehending distress, of children is difficult to bear. It not only makes us vulnerable in working with seriously ill children, but it may cloud our professional judgement. It is only too easy to project one's own thoughts and feelings, fears and fantasies onto the experience of a child, and particularly a terminally ill child. Thus it might be tempting to believe that the child wouldn't want to know the 'awful truth' of his/her impending death; that they are too young to carry such a burden; that they haven't the strength to cope with the unknown, particularly the thought of separation from loved ones for a period of unknown (some would say permanent) duration.

Because regular contact with bereaved families is so emotionally testing and (often) draining, it is important for the practitioner to have his or her own support system available. 'Burnout' is an ever present possibility if practitioners do not care adequately for themselves as well as their patients/clients. The following exercise is designed to help you address this.

Exercise

Discuss these issues with colleagues or think through them for yourself.

1. What are my own – perhaps unacknowledged/denied – thoughts and feelings about death?

2. How do I think about/rationalize/come to terms with a child's death?

3. How might my attitudes get in the way of helping a child and family at the time of a terminal illness?

4. How do I translate my own values/caring emotions into a positive resource for supporting a family at such a difficult time?

The family

Every year approximately 15,000 deaths of children and young people under 20 years of age occur. Children who are ill are twice as likely as healthy children to have behavioural and emotional problems, a fact that puts an additional strain on parents struggling to cope with the illness in its own right. Hilton Davis (1993) points out how each disease presents specific problems to the child and family.

> When children are hurt, ill or disabled, they need physical and personal attention, and this has consequences for all members of the family. At a relatively trivial level, one of the parents has to stop cooking, reading or watching television to see to the child, to cuddle him/her or kiss a bruise better. If the child is sick, parents become worried, arrangements have to be made to look after her/him while one parent takes the other children to school, or they have to make time to go to the GP. Time may be lost from work, and the other children lose attention. Such consequences are a routine part of family life but, in chronic disease, they become a way of life. Anxiety may be the norm, outside commitments may be impossible and childcare duties are increased, including appointments with professionals and even periods away from home for hospital admissions.

Davis describes how parents are profoundly affected by illness in their children, with as many as 33 per cent of parents of children with cancer, even in remission, having such severe depression and anxiety that they require professional help. In a study conducted by Davis and one of his students, 31 per cent of mothers of children with diabetes were found to have stress levels that would have benefited from a professional mental health intervention.

Communication and relationship problems are reflected in increased marital distress, sometimes ending in divorce. There is evidence of increased disturbance in siblings, including irritability, social withdrawal, jealousy and guilt, academic under-achievement, behaviour problems, anxiety and low self-esteem. A major problem is the disturbance of the other children's social relationships, especially with their parents. They tend to feel neglected in comparison with the sick child.

It is plain to see that the social context – 'the family unit' – cannot be overlooked in one's rightful concern about, and priority-giving to, the ill or dying child.

The parents

A diagnosis of serious (perhaps terminal) illness brings about a radical shift in the way parents perceive their child; in other words, the 'stories' they tell themselves about him/her. The previous story of a well child must be reconstructed as a story about an ill child. This requires a huge adjustment in parents' thinking about him/her and this is a process which arouses fear and anxiety. Uncertainty prevails; parents cannot anticipate what will happen to their child. The days, months and years that were taken for granted can no longer be counted on. Children also have to adapt to the disease, cope with the dawning awareness of death, and somehow come to terms with it.

Parents will need to overcome their own difficulties to nurture and communicate openly with the child. Davis believes that the skills of doing this are essentially similar to those used by professionals to communicate with parents so it becomes appropriate that professionals should explicitly share these skills with parents where necessary.

In order to be able to talk to children about death and to answer their questions, health professionals should be aware of how much the child understands about the concept of death itself. We also need to be clear in our work with children that there are marked individual differences in what they understand about dying and death, which are not only due to differences in age, and in the way in which they react to the loss of loved ones. Children as young as three know that death occurs, but they may not grasp the full implications until they are eight or older. Those who have had some experience of death, or who have talked about it, may have a more advanced concept than other children. Adolescents usually have an adult concept of what death means.

Dawning awareness of death

Stages in the concept of illness that contribute to an awareness of death have been outlined as follows (see Clunies-Ross and Lansdowne, 1988).

Stage 1: I am very ill.
Stage 2: I have an illness that can kill people.
Stage 3: I have an illness that can kill children.
Stage 4: I may not get better.
Stage 5: I am dying.

The difficulty with assessing children's knowledge of the concept of death is the dependence on verbal expression. Children who are more verbally competent have a more complete concept of death than those who are not. Nevertheless, it is likely that children are at least aware of the concept of death before they are able to express it adequately.

Researchers have found that when children of different ages were asked, 'Do you believe that some day you will die?', the following percentages were found (see Table 1).

Table 1.   Belief in own mortality

Age in years				
	5	6	7	8–10
% saying yes	50	73	82	100

To summarize, it is only by sensitive conversations with children about death that we can reach an understanding of how much they know and can apply to themselves as children, rather than only to older people.

Part II: Counselling and treatment

Talking to a child who is dying

> A child can live through anything so long as he or she is told the truth and is allowed to share with loved ones the natural feelings people have when they are suffering.
>
> (Eda le Shan: *The Compassionate Friends Newsletter*, Autumn 1987)

The generally held view at present is that parents' wishes should be respected as to whether the child should be told that s/he is dying. Health care professionals are likely to seek permission from parents often reluctant to talk about these issues, or try to encourage them to talk with the child themselves. It is an emotionally fraught situation for everyone concerned when parents refuse to talk openly with their dying child, especially when s/he is asking for information or reassurance.

Points to raise with parents

➢ **The role of parents as models.** Parents are important as role-models in determining the child's response to illness and death. If they can cope with courage and outer calmness, the child is likely to be better able to cope. For some children their particular concern is how their illness and death will affect their parents.

➢ **Resilience in the face of bad news.** A dying child is often far better able to cope with the information of their death than their parents are. Many children are resilient in the face of stress of all kinds.

➢ **Children have rights**. Their need to know the truth (that is, whether it is in their best interests) should be considered very carefully. Advocacy for the child is one of the professional's functions!

Being kept in the dark

Children aware of secrecy may feel isolated, and abandoned by the people they depend on and trust, at a time when they are most vulnerable. They are not 'blind' to non-verbal signals, tones of voice, and 'special' expressions from staff and family. They notice their parents showing extreme worry and sadness, hear their ambiguous, guarded, stilted conversations, and they wish to know what is happening. Children often choose a particular person whom they want to talk to about death and dying. Although some children may not ask questions, it does not necessarily mean they are not preoccupied with concerns about death. After all, they may see the deaths of other children on the ward, or they may know of other children with the same illness where it proved to be fatal.

Whose rights should be given priority – the parents' or the child's? The parents may be unable to face the reality that their child is dying and so will not talk about it, even though the nearness of the end is obvious. Although some parents need to deny the reality of their child's impending death in order to survive emotionally, it is important that this does not become an extra burden for the child. If health care professionals wish to get permission to talk with the child about the subject parents cannot face, they might point out that in giving such a 'go ahead' they are recognizing their child has needs which deserve priority.

Different wards have different policies about whether to tell a child s/he is dying, who should tell, and how to go about such a difficult and delicate task. If parents can be persuaded, children who are questioning and demonstrating that they know they might be dying have the right to have their queries answered clearly and openly. They may be struggling with terrifying fantasies about death, and talking about dying allows such fantasies to be disclosed and (hopefully) defused.

What do I say to the child?

Elisabeth Kübler-Ross (1983) says, 'Although all patients have the *right* to know, not all patients have the *need* to know'. The child may ask questions about death suddenly, out of the blue, catching staff and parents unprepared and off-guard. The resulting consternation may lead to precipitate, ill-judged responses. It is important to be prepared, to be thoughtful and to find out from the child what s/he already knows, what they think or suspect, and **what they really want to know**. The latter is crucial.

Seriously ill children may disclose something that has been on their mind for some time, or an event on the ward, such as another child dying, may precipitate the worried enquiry. This may be the first time the question has been asked. Questions about death might occur in the context of discussions about their illness and treatments, and this is often a useful time at which to address issues. Children who do not understand the answer they are given, or do not get the answer they need, are likely to return repeatedly to the issue that is worrying them.

Reflecting a child's questions back to them is a way of encouraging the expression of feelings. For example, if a child suddenly asks, 'Am I going to die?', the response could be: 'What is it that makes you think you are going to die?' Children may demonstrate a sophisticated understanding about the severity of their illness, or they may simply conclude that something is serious because they saw someone crying or whispering about them. They may not actually be asking about death, but about why their parents are so distressed.

A child's previous experience of death can be another lead into a discussion. If a relative has died, this can introduce the topic. Enquiring about the child's feelings at the time, their knowledge about what happened, and what was said to them, can lead to a conversation about different beliefs and explanations about death. A pet's demise is another way into the subject.

Ideas to help/support the child

- ➤ Make opportunities for conversations while carrying out an activity or playing; talking while playing with the child, doing a craft activity or drawing is one way of being close and comforting.
- ➤ Ask the child how **they** would like support.
- ➤ Let him or her know it's alright to feel afraid, angry, resentful, or in some other way, distressed.
- ➤ Use books/stories/music, especially at night when they are thinking thoughts that make them afraid and morbid.
- ➤ Give time and attention: listen.
- ➤ Tackle the taboo subjects: be honest with questions.
- ➤ Watch for verbalizations and behaviour changes that suggest problems (for example, fear, loneliness, depression).
- ➤ Involve the child's special friends in visits. Discourage social isolation.
- ➤ Provide the occasional opportunity for privacy, a place to express emotions or be quietly alone.

➤   Be sensitive to a child's beliefs: don't deny their viewpoint unless a clearly harmful attitude requires modifying or reframing.

➤   Do picture stories (make sure that useful booklets on illness and death are available – see Further Reading, pp. 34–35).

➤   Suggest at the end that s/he might write goodbye cards/letters/poems to, or draw pictures for, loved ones.

Towards, and at, the end

Inevitably, whatever the preparation and the expectations, it can be a devastating trauma to parents when they finally accept that nothing further can be done for their child. They may deny this, and resist giving up hope. It is important that parents realize the truth of the situation so that they can begin to come to terms with the inevitable and thus be in a position to help and support their child. The strength and sensitivity of the nursing or counselling relationship can be crucial during this period. Parents need time and repeated opportunities to discuss what is happening and to share their views and worries with the professional.

Bereavement (and pre-bereavement) counselling

There seems little doubt that counselling support of various kind mitigates some of the known ill-effects of the trauma of bereavement on physical and mental health.

Hilton Davis has prepared a list of points to be considered with families during illness, or after death, if appropriate. The points focus on the parents, but the helper might apply these objectives to other members of the family, including the child who is ill, the latter with the explicit permission of the parents. Specific objectives of helping are:

➤   to support the parents emotionally and socially throughout the adaptation process, encouraging them in all they do;

➤   to enhance the parents' self-esteem; helping them feel good about themselves;

➤   to increase the parents' feelings of self-efficacy, enabling them to feel in control and able to cope.

➤   to help the parents explore their situation so that they will be more

able to understand and anticipate events, in terms of the disease
and its consequences generally;

➤ to enable the parents to communicate effectively with and support
the child who is ill or disabled, so as to maximize her/his psychological and physical well-being;

➤ to enable parents to develop general coping strategies, allowing them
to analyse problems, determine options and devise ways of dealing
with any situations that may arise;

➤ where there are two parents in the family, to help them feel good
about each other and to encourage open communication and mutual
support;

➤ to enable parents to find their own support systems as necessary
outside the immediate family;

➤ to help parents communicate appropriately with professionals in
order to work in partnership;

➤ to enable the parents to make decisions for themselves, in consultation as necessary, and to foster independence.

Impending death

Once hospital staff and family have accepted that the end is near,
preparations and decisions can be made about how to best care for
the child and family. If treatment has come to an end and the issue of
death has not yet been raised by the child, it will be necessary to
discuss with the parents how to raise it. Some children may not have
even thought of it, while others may be fully aware. As death draws
nearer, the child and the parents need to have the opportunity to say
goodbye and to complete any final tasks. The child may want to return
home for a last time to say goodbye to their house and toys, or they
may request that certain toys and possessions be brought to the
hospital. The extended family may want to say goodbye. The child
may wish to write a letter or draw a special picture for friends or
classmates to be remembered by, or to remember them by. It is
important to ask the child if there is anything they feel they still need
to do, and whether they have any special requests or need any special
help.

Once the decision has been made that a child is to be supported
only on medication to ease pain, if present, the possibility of the
child going home is often raised. Parents may be unable, emotionally,
to make decisions and plans, but most parents prefer to have their
child at home in familiar surroundings for as long as possible.

At the end

(See also Douglas (1993) for a helpful guide.)

When the child dies, health professionals should check with the parents whether they prefer company or privacy while with their child. Parents might be encouraged to touch the dead child and cuddle the body if they want to. It is essential at this stage for parents to feel that they have time with their child, without being rushed or feeling that they are inconveniencing staff. Families need to be told that siblings might wish to see the dead child, as sometimes their feelings are overlooked. It can help the process of grieving if everyone has a chance to say goodbye, and to say what they wish, to the dead child. Younger children may like to draw a goodbye card for their brother or sister.

Once arrangements have been made for the transfer of the child's body to the funeral directors, the parents go home, very much alone with their loss. This is often their last visit to the hospital, where they may have spent many months during the child's illness. Ward staff have been involved in the care of the child, and it is important to the families that nurses show concern after death as well as before it. The loss of contact with ward staff and the hospital itself can be an additional loss for the parents whose lives may have been totally occupied with visiting their ill child. Some hospitals have ward–home liaison teams which provide continued care in the community, supporting the family and community health care staff.

Liaison with community services is essential to help the parents feel supported away from the hospital; families may have become dependent on the hospital during a long and drawn out treatment programme lasting many months, or even years.

Siblings' vulnerability

Siblings are sometimes overlooked when there is a bereavement in the family. Children are at risk of what I call a 'double jeopardy': the loss, not only of a sibling, but a temporary 'loss' of their grieving, pre-occupied care-giver(s). They may feel rejected and abandoned and grandparents' care and solidity at such times (and, indeed, that of older siblings and other relatives) may be crucial, and therefore should not be forgotten in your work with bereaved parents.

Given the vital importance of children's emotional attachments to the family, the loss of a sibling is a particularly poignant experience.

We need a good knowledge base about the nature and development of children's grief if we are to be effective in counselling bereaved children and their parents (these matters are dealt with in Part IV).

To help families come to terms with the death you need to help them:

> to accept the loss;
> to express their feelings/emotions;
> to accept their feelings as normal;
> to live without the loved one;
> to deal with 'tasks' that families have to get on with in life;
> to clarify distortions and misconceptions;
> to cope with family changes;

You will also need to:

> help the sibling to cope and understand the surviving parent's grief;
> help the parents to cope and understand the child's grief;
> encourage 'healing family tasks'. This implies:
>   • a shared knowledge of the reality of death and shared experience of loss; and,
>   • reorganization of the family system and reinvestment in other relationships and life pursuits.

Encourage the parents and surviving children to communicate with each other. Explore, using conversation, play, drawing, genograms and stories, how siblings who are bereaved are thinking, feeling and coping. This will tell you the 'coping tasks' they are working on. We need to look sensitively at the 'stories' they are telling themselves about why their brother or sister died.

Most bereaved persons are feeling 'better' at the end of the first year following the loss, but the child's grieving process generally takes approximately two years in all, as for adults. Of course, this does not preclude the return of the pain of sadness and yearning, especially at anniversary and holiday time.

Part III: Bereavement in adults and children

Introduction

Children are sometimes forgotten and overlooked when there is a bereavement in the family. This is not to imply a callous disregard for their feelings, but rather an ignorance of what they feel in the face of death, or an inability to 'read' their innermost thoughts and emotions from their behaviour (or the absence of certain kinds of behaviour one expects after a bereavement). This applies especially to very young children.

It is vital, when thinking about how to help bereaved children, that the family context is not dealt with superficially. What children understand about death and the way they react to the loss of loved ones depend significantly on what they have been taught and experienced within the family, and the role-models of surviving parents and relatives in coping with loss.

Given the limitations of children's understanding of the world and the immaturity of their coping strategies, the loss of a parent is a particularly far-reaching experience. Sadly, the resources for supporting/counselling bereaved children are thin on the ground although the need is great. Statistics show that **every day** in the United Kingdom, approximately 550 wives become widows, 150 husbands become widowers, and almost 40 children under 14 die.

In all, some 180,000 children under 16 have lost a mother or father through death. Of these bereaved children, approximately 120,000 are widows' children and 60,000 are widowers' children. The loss of a parent is one of the foremost precursors of depressive disorders. In order to help children cope with the loss of a parent, we need to understand how and when their reactions are both normal and necessary.

There is little doubt that children's reactions to death and their ability to cope with the immediate shock of losing a parent, and later to adjust so as to get on with growing up and living, is influenced greatly by the reactions of the surviving parent.

Dora Black (1993) has this to say:

> There is much evidence that if we do not grieve at the time we are likely to be affected throughout our lives in all kinds of subtle ways. If children do not mourn, their personal development may be constricted. Adults who fail to mourn are likely to deal with issues of loss, even minor loss, in maladaptive ways.

Before we look specifically at the way children grieve, it is essential to examine the process of bereavement of the adult who continues to care for the child. First, we need to be clear about our terminology. Colin Murray Parkes suggests the following definitions.

> ➤ **Bereavement**: the situation of anyone who has lost a person to whom they are attached.
> ➤ **Grief**: the psychological and emotional reactions to bereavement.
> ➤ **Mourning**: the social face of grief.
> ➤ **Attachment**: a strong tendency to remain close to, or from time to time, to return to, another individual.
> ➤ **Anticipatory grief**: the psychological and emotional reaction to the anticipation of bereavement.

Grieving adults

Several authors have described a 'normal' or 'uncomplicated' pattern of grieving in the first year following a death. An understanding of these processes should help us to avoid the temptation to 'pathologize' the bereaved individual's reactions. The progression is not necessarily inevitable or uniform for everyone, or indeed, for any one person.

Uncomplicated grieving

Phase 1: Numbness. This occurs close to the time of the loss. It may be associated with **shock** and **disbelief/denial**. These reactions are most pronounced when the death is unexpected.

Phase 2: Yearning. The bereaved person yearns for the lost person to return as indicated by **crying**, **searching**, **reminiscence**, **anger**, **guilt** and **hallucinatory experiences**. This is, perhaps, the 'heart' of grief and the earliest memories of painful separation may be reawakened at this time. It is a time of acute and aching pain and distress. It is manifested in the days following the upsurge of death and after the flourish of activity and human contact that accompany the funeral.

Phase 3: Disorganization and despair. The person finds it difficult to get on with life because of feelings of hopelessness, helplessness, loneliness, anxiety and depression. Some theorists feel that Phases 2 and 3 merge. There is a sense of threat to the bereaved person's security, identity and purpose, brought about by the loss of a significant bond of love and dependency.

Phase 4: Reorganization. There is an acceptance of the loss and a feeling of getting one's life together again. The pain of grief is less acute, the sense of loss not so unbearable, so intolerable. The point has been made that it is not so much that 'time is a great healer', but that time (which means life) goes on and holds so much to occupy, challenge and attract the breaved. The past loses its hold, although it is not forgotten. The person reformulates his/her identity and life without the deceased.

It is important to realize that the stages described may merge, be missed out or repeated, if the person regresses.

Black (1993) provides a telling analogy of these processes of grief with the behaviour of a small child lost in a supermarket when accidentally separated from her mother:

> After the first shocked realisation that she is lost the child will start agitatedly running up and down all the aisles of the supermarket seeking for her mother, crying loudly to attract her attention. If she fails to be reunited eventually the agitation ceases and tears of grief begin. During the reunion much anger is expressed.

Complicated grieving

In a proportion of cases, adults' grief may be complicated, indeed pathological, in the following ways:

- ➤ a failure to mourn;
- ➤ grief is delayed;
- ➤ grief is prolonged interminably (shading into clinical depression);
- ➤ grief is distorted (for example, by extreme self-recrimination, guilt or anger).

Why grieving may be abnormal

There are certain features in the type of death, the kind of relationship and in the surviving partner's personality which make a complicated grieving more likely (see Ward *et al.,* 1993). Table 2 outlines these.

Table 2.   Features leading to abnormal grieving

	Features
Type of death	Survivor may be to blame; death sudden; death unexpected; death untimely; death painful; death horrific; death mismanaged.
Nature of relationship	Dependent or symbiotic; ambivalent; a spouse who dies; a child under 20 who dies; a parent (particularly a mother) who dies.
Survivor's attributes	A grief-prone personality; insecure; overanxious; low self-esteem; previous mental illness; excessively angry; excessively self-reproachful; physically disabled; unable to express grief; previous loss.

Grieving children

We need to be clear in our work with bereaved children that there are marked *individual differences* in what they understand about dying and death and the way in which they react to the loss of loved ones. We cannot work in a prescriptive, 'formula' manner. Each child and every family is unique and must be considered in their own right, but against a background of a thorough knowledge of the literature on bereavement and how it affects children at different stages of development.

Development of the concept of death

The way in which children make sense of (or fail to comprehend) death and grief is related to their cognitive, emotional and physical stages of development. The information below is based on empirical studies (see Kane, 1979). It is necessary to remember that it is based upon generalizations to which there are exceptions, especially with regard to differences in life-experience and individual differences in the rate of development.

Children under four years of age

1.   *Cognitive factors*:
➢   The 'preconceptual stage' of cognitive development lasts from about two to four years of age (Piaget, 1929). At this stage children's

concepts are not fully formed – they don't understand, for example, the permanence of death. Because their thinking is prelogical and often 'magical' (the notion that some things and people have power over others; the child experiencing him/herself as at the centre of things), misconceptions and misinterpretations of the 'world' they live in can be a problem. Another source of worry to the child is their misinterpretation of causality. The immature kind of thinking called 'psychological causality' refers to the tendency in young children to attribute a **psychological motive** as the cause of events. For example, children may think that a parent has gone to hospital because he or she is angry with them, rather than due to illness.

➤ Distress on separation implies attachment to the person. The mean age of the onset of attachment is in the third quarter of the first year (notably 6–8 months).

➤ Very young children (most three-year-olds and even younger children) are **aware** of death and are familiar with the word 'death' before they enter school.

➤ Their ability to **conceptualize** death and its implications is very limited. For example, because they do not understand that death is final, they may search for the departed parent and pester the surviving one ('When is Mummy/Daddy coming back?').

➤ Children develop a realistic concept of death gradually; new components of understanding are 'added in' so as eventually to bring about a full grasp of its realities (see Kane, 1979). Hopefully, much of this learning occurs as children encounter 'small bereavements' such as a pet's death. Truthful, factual explanations of death, given in a calm manner, provide them with a grasp of reality, which will help their adjustment to later, more personal, losses such as the death of a grandparent.

2. *Emotional factors:*

➤ At this early stage, children's emotional reactions to the disappearance of a parent, for whatever cause, tend to be similar. Children of barely four years of age can yearn for departed parents, and wait for their return.

➤ John Bowlby makes the point that children older than a few weeks or months display the same **separation anxiety** whether the parent is away for a few hours or for considerably longer.

➤ Young children cannot sustain a sad mood for prolonged periods of time.

➤ They cannot **differentiate** feelings as finely as older children.

3.   *Physical factors:*
➤   Children who are too young to make themselves understood through speech may react physically to the bereavement by:
   • wetting
   • loss of appetite
   • disturbed sleep
   • clinging behaviour
   • catching infections

Children aged five to ten years of age

1.   *Cognitive factors:*
➤   The intuitive stage of thinking (4–7 years) moves the child on from the preconceptual stage (2–4) mentioned earlier, and they develop the ability to classify, order and quantify things, while still remaining unaware of the principles which underlie these abilities. It is only in the next stage of **concrete operations** (7 plus) that these principles become more explicit, so that children can explain their logical reasoning in a satisfactory way.
➤   Before 6 or 7 children often attribute life to inanimate objects.
➤   It is between the age of 7 and 9 that there appears to be a nodal point in children's development of concepts about life and death. By about 7 most children have a fairly clear idea of 'life' and a more or less complete concept of 'death'. It shouldn't be forgotten that many 5-year-olds have a fairly full concept.
➤   When children are about 8–9 they realize that dying can apply to themselves.

   Kane (1979) describes the child's understanding of death between the ages of 5 and 10 in terms of the components he or she is cognitively capable of comprehending, as follows:

➤   **Separation** (understood by most five-year-olds). Young children can be very aware that death means separation from their parents, friends or brothers and sisters. This may be the main concept they focus on, and they may be concerned that they will feel lonely or that their parents will be lonely without them.
➤   **Immobility** (understood by most five-year-olds). The awareness that dead people cannot move can concern some children who are not also aware that dead people cannot feel, see or hear.
➤   **Irrevocability** (understood by most six-year-olds). The fact that once people die they cannot come back to life again is essential in understanding death. Many children younger than five or six may

not realize the finality of the process. Children play games about being shot and dying, but then leap to life the next minute. 'Pretend' death and 'real' death need to be made clear, so that the child realizes that 'real' death means never living again.

➤ **Causality** (understood by most six-year-olds). There is always a physical cause of death. Young children, however, often have unusual or 'magical' ideas about what causes death. For example, a nasty wish, saying something horrible or being naughty can sometimes be perceived as having caused illness or death. Children need to understand that it is not such imaginary events the cause death, but that something is wrong with the body that causes people to die.

➤ **Dysfunctionality** (understood by most six-year-olds). Explanations about death to children should include the cessation of bodily functions, for example, that the body stops breathing, growing, seeing, hearing, thinking and feeling, and the heart stops beating. Some children worry that they might be able to hear what is happening to themselves but not be able to tell anyone.

➤ **Universality** (understood by most seven-year-olds). That every living organism dies at some time is important in understanding that everyone must die eventually. This idea can comfort some children who may believe that everyone lives forever and that it is unfair that they, or someone they close to, are dying.

➤ **Insensitivity** (understood by most eight-year-olds). That a dead person cannot feel anything is often difficult for young children to understand. For example, if they walk on a grave they may wonder if they are 'hurting' the person under the ground. One way of helping a child who is dying in pain, or who has parents who have been in pain, is to help them to realize they will never feel pain again after death. (The conceptual development of children with a serious illness – leukaemia – is not overall significantly different from that of healthy children (Clunies-Ross and Lansdowne, 1988).)

2. *Emotional factors:*
➤ Disturbances of emotion and behaviour are common. In one study, 50 per cent of children studied manifested problems such as school refusal, stealing and poor concentration one year after the loss of a parent, with 30 per cent displaying problems after two years.

Adolescents

1. *Cognitive factors:*
➤ **Appearance** of the dead is understood by most 12-year-olds. A

dead body looks different to a living body, and children may be very interested in the physical characteristics of death. They can seem ghoulish sometimes in their desire for detailed descriptions of what a dead person looks like.

➤ Adolescents, like adults, realize the permanence of death and therefore tend to look for meanings: the big 'Why?' questions.

➤ The adolescent's thinking is flexible. S/he is capable of abstract thought, can hypothesize and work things out (principles etc.) for themselves. Thus, they may have their own theories about death and question cherished beliefs about, say, the afterlife, in a way that dismays the surviving parent.

2.   *Emotional factors:*

➤ Adolescents express their grief more like adults.

➤ The development task of separating from parents may be delayed (particularly for eldest children or those who are the same sex as the deceased parent). The adolescent's search for identity may be influenced by his/her answers to the 'why' questions referred to previously.

➤ Some adolescents display an apparent lack of feeling or indifference owing (it is postulated) to conflicts between the drives toward independence and continuing dependence (referred to previously).

Potential problems

➤ Although some very young children have an almost complete concept of death, the individual differences, especially for the under-eights, are very large.

➤ Children have difficulty in calling up memories when very young. (Photograph albums are helpful here in recalling family events.)

➤ They find it difficult to imagine that they will miss the parent at times such as anniversaries and holidays, and are thus unprepared for the distress when these occasions come around.

➤ Their egocentricity and literal-mindedness might cause them to blame themselves for the parent's death and departure.

➤ They may have fantasies about being reunited with the loved person.

➤ They may wish to 'die' in order to be reunited with the loved person.

➤ Illusions or hallucinations of seeing the parent (a common experience in adults too) may be taken to be real.

➤ Children's 'playing out' of dying and death may seem callous and inappropriate to the adult observer who is unaware of the function of play.

➤ Children may have difficulties of concentration and other learning difficulties at school following a bereavement.

➤ They only gradually develop the capacity to sustain feelings of sadness over a period of time, and may be misinterpreted as being unfeeling.

➤ They may feel embarrassed at being 'different' (having lost a parent) at school.

➤ They may feel anxious about losing the other parent.

➤ They may worry about who is going to feed them and look after them in other ways.

Part IV: The child's reactions to death

There are many influences ('multiple variables') affecting children's reactions to the death of a parent, sibling, or some other significant person. There is, therefore, no place for simplistic or dogmatic predictions as to how a particular child from a particular family will respond.

But parents are likely to confront the counsellor with the question: 'Are my child's reactions normal?', so knowledge of 'normal' grieving is essential. Beyond that, the counsellor's role and strategy are likely to be multidimensional and systemic. This means that there are several levels at which he or she may have to focus their attentions, and certainly on the system of relationships between, and responses from, members of the family and possibly also on the system of support (or otherwise) from the school and neighbourhood.

Emotional reactions of the child

Children vary markedly in the way they react initially to the news of death. Many weep copiously, while some react hardly at all on the surface. Sometimes children don't know how to react because they don't understand what has happened (usually due to a lack of honest information).

The emotional reactions may include the following:

➤ shock and denial ('I don't believe it!');
➤ anger ('How can God do this to us?');
➤ guilt ('Why did/didn't I ... ? If only I had ...');
➤ jealousy ('How is it they haven't lost their mum?');
➤ sadness/loneliness ('I miss Dad so much; why can't he come back?');
➤ high anxiety ('Who will take care of me?');
➤ withdrawal (frozen/wooden/apathetic);
➤ exaggerated separation responses, such as clinging behaviour;
➤ excessive crying;
➤ markedly aggressive behaviour;
➤ sleep disturbance;

> ➤ disorders of eating;
> ➤ disorders of toileting;
> ➤ other habit disorders;
> ➤ other physical symptoms.

What may go wrong?

> ➤ **Oversight**. These reactions are frequently missed by parents. In Beverley Raphael's (1982) study of 35 children aged 2–8 (21 girls, 14 boys), for 40 per cent of the children there was a denial by the surviving parent that the children showed any response to the loss, or that they were affected by it, despite clear evidence to the contrary.
> ➤ **Being kept in the dark.** Children are likely to be adversely affected if they don't comprehend what is happening, or has happened. Complications may arise because they are given inaccurate information owing to taboos about death or an adult's inability to face the finality of death, leading to a denial of what has happened.
> ➤ **Unhelpful explanations.** Children, when young, have difficulties with abstract explanations. As we have seen above, their thinking is concrete and literal. If the dead parent is now a 'star in heaven', 'asleep' or 'on a journey', the explanation may turn out to be counterproductive and confusing. But it has to be said that the relationship between misconceptions about death and longer term outcomes is still unknown.
> ➤ **The role of parents as models.** Parents are important as role models in determining the child's response to the death. Sometimes the child's lack of pining, yearning and sadness can be traced to the parent's reactions, or absence of them.
> ➤ **Fantasies and causal thinking.** Children's fantasies and causal thinking may have an adverse influence on their grieving. Some children have fantasies about the hospital being a place where children are taken to die.
> ➤ **Relationship with the dead person.** An unhappy or ambivalent relationship with the deceased individual can complicate the child's grief, increasing the likelihood of its being pathological (for example, involving shame).
> ➤ **Lack of support.** This is a critical factor, be it due to caregiving failures, economic hardship, the remaining parent's helplessness, anger, depression, preoccupation, pathology, etc. A parent's preoccupation may be interpreted as rejection by the child.

> **Personality.** Some children are resilient in the face of stress of all kinds, for reasons that are still poorly understood (see Herbert, 1991). Others are vulnerable, especially if their previous experiences of loss and separation have not led to a satisfactory resolution and 'healing'.

> **Nature of the death.** Sudden, unexpected death has a greater impact on the survivor than an anticipated death (such as those following a long illness, or from old age). A violent death (especially if witnessed) may lead to complications such as symptoms of post-traumatic stress disorder.

Risk

We have already seen that the loss of a parent is one of the foremost precursors of depressive problems. Losing a parent of the same sex (particularly for boys) appears to be a particularly significant risk factor for depression. The results of research suggest several risk factors for poor adjustment, including the following:

> mental illness in the surviving parent;
> financial difficulties after the death of a parent;
> the sex of the child and of the surviving parent;
> the stability of the home environment prior to and/or after the death;
> the quality of the marital relationship before the death;
> the coping capacity of the surviving parent;
> the quality of the support system of the family after the death. It has been shown that the risk of depression increases in the absence of a close, confiding relationship.

There seems little doubt that counselling support of various kind mitigates some of the known ill-effects of the trauma of bereavement on physical and mental health. Children are remarkable, **if they have a secure base**, in the way they seem to accept the sad facts of life and death and get on with living. A simple, straightforward explanation of the death is better than a dishonest palliative which mystifies the child. An awesome silence about the dead person will not help the child to work through and resolve grief.

Loss through divorce/the break-up of partnerships

Bereavement is not, of course, limited to the loss of loved ones through death. The loss of parents, or separation from one of them, due to the termination of relationships, is a common experience in western society today. In Britain, at least one in five children will have experienced the effects of divorce by the time they are 16 years old. It is a sad fact of life that, in general, the outcomes of divorce for children are more emotionally damaging than those for death.

When should I refer on?

You may meet children whose reactions give you cause for concern and you have to decide whether to seek additional help. Following are some signs which may help you make such a decision. Consider referring on to a child and family consultation centre, or discussing your concerns with a specialist if:

> the bereaved child looks sad all the time, apathetic and downcast, with **prolonged** depression;
> the child is pretending nothing has happened;
> the child feels worthless and makes remarks of bitter self-recrimination;
> s/he becomes indifferent to interests and hobbies (and school activities) once enjoyed;
> s/he becomes indifferent to how s/he looks and dresses;
> s/he seems tired, unable to sleep, with their health suffering;
> the child threatens, or talks of suicide;
> s/he becomes persistently aggressive;
> s/he becomes markedly and persistently withdrawn and socially isolated (avoids social activities/wishes to be alone all of the time);
> the child becomes involved with antisocial acts such as drugs/stealing, etc.;
> the child begins to live at a fast, jittery tempo/pace and can't relax at all with parents, siblings or friends;
> suicide was the cause of death, as this can be especially difficult for the child.

Part V: Helping bereaved clients

Bereavement counselling

Counselling is based on a relationship of trust and confidential conversations between the professionally trained counsellor and the client. Carl Rogers played a major part in developing the client-centred, non-directive approach as akin to education – a learning process within a humanistic context. The attributes of the counsellor which facilitate such learning are thought to be:

> ➤ **Genuineness and authenticity**: the conveying of realness to the client.
> ➤ **Non-possessive warmth**: an attitude of friendly but unintrusive concern and caring.
> ➤ **Accurate empathy**: the capacity to see things from the clients' point of view; to 'feel with' them so that **they** feel understood.

Counselling, within this framework, involves the painstaking but gentle exploration of issues and problems in an attempt to clarify confusing or conflicting issues and to discover ways (possibly alternative ones) of describing them and/or of dealing with them. They might involve feelings of guilt about things said (or unsaid) to the dead; feelings aroused, such as relief, anger and resentment, which seem 'inappropriate'; or fantasies that block the process of grieving.

This helping method, based on a **collaborative** model of working (Herbert, 1993), emphasizes the 'self-help' element, the need to call on the inner resources of the child and parent. To this end the counsellor provides a non-judgemental, supportive relationship which enables individuals to enhance their self-esteem, self-respect and self-efficacy (confidence), in part by learning to search for their **own** answers and to rely on their own resources.

Empowering clients

Providing information is a crucial component in the empowerment of clients; this is particularly the case with children facing the potential and actual loss of a loved caregiver. Relating this helping process to the parent with a bereaved child (children) might involve adopting (*inter alia*) the following broad aims.

➤   To facilitate the ways in which the parent and other members of the family grieve and adapt to the death, psychologically, socially, physically and in their everyday lives, minimizing or preventing disruption as far as possible.

➤   To enable family members as best they can to meet the needs of the bereaved person without neglecting their own needs.

➤   To enable the child who is grieving to have the best possible quality of life by facilitating his/her adaptation to the loss, psychologically, socially and in the tasks and pursuits of everyday life (children have different developmental tasks at different stages of life which, if not coped with adequately, may have consequences that are distressing and damaging (Herbert, 1993)).

There is evidence (for example, Herbert, 1991; Murray Parkes, 1983) that working with the family is an effective way of helping bereaved children. When working specifically with the child, discuss your involvement and concerns with the parent. Don't lose contact with him/her; follow-up sessions ('boosters') may be required.

Objectives of the counselling intervention

The specific objectives you need to think about in order to meet the aims described above might be as follows:

1.   Allow/help the child to grieve; that is, 'give permission'. It is rare for children to be given the opportunity to grieve. Dora Black puts it as follows:

> People avoid talking to children about a dead parent, misconceptions persist, and the child gets little chance of accurately restructuring his world view.

2.   To help children come to terms with their loss you need to help them:
   *   to accept the loss;
   *   to express their feelings/emotions;
   *   to accept their feelings as normal;
   *   to live without the loved one (this may mean practical help for the family);
   *   to deal with developmental tasks that move them on towards maturity and independence;

- to clarify distortions and misconceptions;
- to cope with family changes.

3.   Help the child to cope with and understand the surviving parent's grief; help the parent to cope with and understand the child's grief.

4.   Explore (using conversation, play, drawing, genograms, and stories) how children are thinking, feeling and acting. This will tell you the 'grief tasks' they are working on. We need to look sensitively at the 'stories' they are telling us.

Some dos for the helper

➢   Be available to the family; keep in touch.

➢   Listen ... 'give permission' to them to express as much of their sadness as they are willing to share at the time.

➢   Encourage them to talk about their loss.

➢   Normalize their feelings; accept them; explain to them (if necessary).

➢   Be honest and open with questions. Say 'I don't know' when you don't know the answer.

➢   Ask children what help/support they would like.

➢   Ask parents what help/support they would like.

➢   Share, by talking, good and not-so-good family memories (for example, look at family photograph albums with them).

➢   Be aware of previous bereavements.

➢   Be sensitive to special occasions (for example, anniversaries, sickness, holidays).

➢   Encourage the parent to communicate to the child the fact that s/he is not alone: 'I am with you'.

Some don'ts for the helper

➢   Don't advise them not to worry or not to be sad.

➢   Don't advise them as to what they should feel.

➢   Don't say you **know** how they feel ... you don't!

➢   Don't say 'You should be feeling better now'.

➢   Don't say 'At least you still have a mother/father'.

➢   Don't deny their point of view (for example, religious beliefs) when it comes to value issues.

➢   Don't encourage parents to hide their grief from their child. Say: 'It's alright to cry in front of your child'.

➢   Don't say 'Your daddy fell asleep and did not wake up'.
➢   Don't neglect to liaise with the school. Children, when bereaved, may 'misbehave' ('act out') and/or underachieve due to poor concentration, apathy, low motivation (as part of a feeling of depression). Teachers may not be fully aware of the reasons.

Ideas to help/support the child

➢   Let him or her know it's alright to laugh and have fun as well as to grieve.
➢   Ask the child how they would like support.
➢   Give time and attention: listen.
➢   Tackle the taboo subjects: be honest with questions.
➢   Watch for verbalizations and behaviour changes that suggest problems (for example, self-blame, persistent depression).
➢   Involve the child's special friends.
➢   Be mindful of special days.
➢   Provide boltholes for privacy, a place to express emotions or be quietly alone.
➢   Be sensitive to a child's beliefs: don't deny their viewpoint.
➢   Suggest better concentration strategies.
➢   Suggest s/he might write letters/poetry to a loved one.
➢   Do picture stories.
➢   Create a special album.
➢   Normalize their thoughts/feelings.
➢   Make a memorial.

Some dos for the school

Long and Bates (undated book *Loss and Separation*) suggest several ways in which schools can help bereaved children: certainly, they need to be aware of, and sensitive to, the child's grief as it may manifest itself as restlessness and poor attention in the classroom; the disruption of home life may cause the child to be absent from school and/or remiss over homework. What is usually supportive about school life is the predictable routine, stability, safety and focused (distracting) tasks it provides.

As **listeners**, teachers and school counsellors can provide the child with:

➤ the time to talk;
➤ a trusting relationship in which to be heard and supported;
➤ understanding when the child is preoccupied, silent or tearful;
➤ a sense of being valued and 'normal' when they feel isolated and different;
➤ practical support (for example, over learning difficulties).

References

Black, D. (1993). Untitled contribution in B. Ward and Associates, *Good Grief: Exploring Feelings, Loss and Death*. (Vol. 1 with under elevens; Vol. 2 with over elevens and adults.) London: Jessica Kingsley Publishers Ltd.

Clunies-Ross, C. and Lansdowne, R. (1988). Concepts of death, illness and isolation found in children with leukaemia. *Child Care, Health and Development, 14,* 373–386.

Davis, H. (1993). *Counselling Parents of Children with Chronic Illness or Disability.* Leicester: BPS Books (The British Psychological Society).

Douglas, J. (1993). *Psychology and Nursing Children.* Leicester: BPS Books (The British Psychological Society) and Macmillan.

Dyregrov, A. (1992). *Grief in Children: A Handbook for Adults.* London: Jessica Kingsley Publishers Ltd.

Fleming, S. and Balmer, L. (1991). Group intervention with bereaved children. In: D. Papadatou and C. Papadatou (Eds) *Children and Death.* London: Hemisphere.

Furman, E. (1974). *The Child's Parent Dies.* New Haven: Yale University Press.

Grollman, E.A. (1991). *Talking About Death: A Dialogue Between Parent and Child* (revised edn). Boston: Beacon Press.

Herbert, M. (1991). *Clinical Child Psychology: Social Learning, Behaviour and Development.* Chichester: John Wiley.

Herbert, M. (1993). *Working with Children and The Children Act.* Leicester: BPS Books (The British Psychological Society).

Hewett, C. (1984). *Helping Children Cope with Separation and Loss.* London: Batsford.

Kane, B. (1979). Children's concepts of death. *Journal of Genetic Psychology, 134,* 141–145.

Krementz, J. (1983). *How it Feels When a Parent Dies.* London: Gallancz.

Kübler-Ross, E. (1982). *Living with Death and Dying.* New York: Souvenir.

Kübler-Ross, E. (1983). *On Children and Death.* New York: Macmillan

Long, R. and Bates, J. (undated). *Loss and Separation.* Devon Psychological Services.

Murgatroyd, S. (1988). *Counselling and Helping.* London: Methuen and BPS Books.

Murray Parkes, C. (1983). *Recovery from Bereavement.* New York: Basic Books.

Papadatou, D. and Papadatou, C. (Eds) (1991). *Children and Death.* London: Hemisphere.

Piaget, J. (1929). *The Child's Conception of the World.* London: Routledge and Kegan Paul.

Pincus, L. (1961). *Death and the Family.* London: Faber.

Raphael, B. (1982). The young child and the death of a parent. In C. Murray Parkes and J. Stevenson-Hinde (Eds), *The Place of Attachment in Human Behaviour.* New York: Basic Books.

Ward, B. and Associates (1993). *Good Grief: Exploring Feelings, Loss and Death.* (Vol. 1 with under elevens; Vol. 2 with over elevens and adults.) London: Jessica Kingsley Publications Ltd.

Wass, H. (1989). Children and death. In R. Kastenbaum and B. Kastenbaum (Eds), *Encyclopedia of Death.* Phoenix, AZ: Oryx Press.

Further reading

Grandparents

Ponzette, J.J. and Johnson, M.A. (1991). The forgotten grievers: grandparents' reactions to the death of grandchildren. *Death studies, 15,* 157–167.

Adolescents

Fanos, J.H. and Nickerson, B.G. (1991). Long-term effects of sibling death during adolescence. Special issue: death and adolescent bereavement. *Journal of Adolescent Research, 6(1),*70–82.

Harris, E.S. (1991). Adolescent bereavement following the death of a parent. An exploratory study. *Child Psychiatry and Human development, 21(4),* 267–281.

Hogan, N.S., Balk, D.E. (1990). Adolescent reactions to sibling death: perceptions of mothers, fathers and teenagers. *Nursing Research, 39(2),* 103–106.

Pre-school children

Kranzier, E.M., Shaffer, D., Wasserman, G. and Davies, M. (1990). Early childhood bereavement. *Journal of the American Academy of Child and Adolescent Psychiatry, 29(4)*, 513–520.

Nader, K., Stuber, M. and Pynoos, R. (1991). Post-traumatic stress reactions in pre-school children with catastrophic illness: assessment needs. *Comprehensive Mental Health Care, 1*, 223–239.

Siblings

Powell, M. (1991). The psychosocial impact of sudden infant death syndrome on siblings. *Irish Journal of Psychology, 12(2)*, 235–247.

Reactions to death

Raphael, B. (1982). The young child and the death of a parent. In C.Murray Parkes and J. Stevenson-Hinde (Eds), *The Place of Attachment in Human Behaviour.* New York: Basic Books.

Silverman, P.R. and Warden, J. W. (1992). Children's reactions in the early months after the death of a parent. *American Journal of Orthopsychiatry, 62(1)*, 93–104.

Seriously ill children

Clunies-Ross, C. and Lansdowne, R. (1988). Concepts of death, illness and isolation found in children with leukaemia. *Child Care, Health and Development, 14*, 373–386.

General

Marris, P. (1974) *Loss and Change*. London: Routledge and Kegan Paul.

Murray Parkes, C., Relf M., and Couldrick, A. (in press). *Counselling in Terminal Care and Bereavement*. Leicester: BPS Books (The British Psychological Society).

Niven, N. and Robinson, J. (1994). *The Psychology of Nursing Care*. Basingstoke: Macmillan and BPS Books.

Hints for Parents

At times of a bereavement in the family, the grieving child can sometimes be overlooked. This is not due to a lack of concern or sensitivity on the part of the parents, but possibly the misunderstanding of the ways in which children understand (or fail to comprehend) what death means and the different ways in which they react to a bereavement – sometimes like adults, but often quite differently. Their responses or muted reactions may be due to their ignorance of what is happening. Children need to know, in terms that they understand, the meaning of significant events, such as the serious illness or loss of a loved one, that affect the family. Sadly, when there is a bereavement, the child not only loses a beloved member of the family, but also, temporarily, the full attention of the grieving and preoccupied parent. The support of parents for the grieving child, manifested notably in a sharing of information with their child, will help him or her to work through their sadness. It is vital to help children to grieve because a failure to do so may have adverse emotional consequences later in life. You may find the following guidelines helpful.

Some dos and don'ts for the parent

> Do allow children to go through their own individual stages of grief.
> Do seek help from other supportive persons.
> Do notify the child's school or day care centre about the child's bereavement.
> Do encourage children to participate in the family sorrow.
> Do consider grief support groups for children.
> Do provide continued assurance of love and support (when words fail, touch).
> Don't discourage the subject of death in the home, the school, the church or other place of worship.
> Don't discourage the emotional express of grief.
> Don't tell children something they will later need to unlearn (for example, that the dead person is sleeping).

➤ Don't alter the role of the child (for example, making them a replacement for the dead person).
➤ Don't speak beyond a child's level of comprehension.